The Dog Walker's Handbook

Tips and Tricks for Starting and Operating a Dog Walking Business

EmptyInkwell

Copyright © 2024 EmptyInkwell

All rights reserved.

ISBN: 9798324180669

EXTRA INCOME

A Practical Guide to Earning More with Simple Side Hustles

TABLE OF CONTENTS

Why Start a Dog Walking Service?	**1**
How to Plan Your Dog Walking Service	**5**
How to Market Your Dog Watching Service	**12**
How to Operate Your Dog Walking Service	**18**
How to Grow Your Dog Walking Service	**22**
How to Succeed as a Dog Walker	**28**

WHY START A DOG WALKING SERVICE?

Starting a dog walking service has many benefits. Not only can you make money, but you also get to work with animals, be your own boss, and have flexible hours.

There are some common myths and misconceptions about dog walking, such as that it is easy, boring, or low paying. However, the demand and potential of dog walking is high. There are many dog owners, and the average spending on pet services is significant. The industry is also growing at a steady rate.

Many dog walkers have made a living or even a fortune from their business. Success stories and testimonials from these dog walkers can provide inspiration and motivation for starting your own dog walking service.

Benefits of Starting a Dog Walking Service

Starting a dog walking service can be a rewarding and fulfilling experience. Here are some of the benefits of starting a dog walking service:

Make Money: Dog walking can be a lucrative business. With the right marketing and pricing strategies, you can generate a steady income from your dog walking service. You can also increase your earnings by offering additional services, such as pet sitting or dog training.

Work with Animals: If you love animals, especially dogs, then starting a dog walking service can be a dream come true. You get to spend time with dogs, take them for walks, and provide them with love and care. It can be a fulfilling and enjoyable experience.

Be Your Own Boss: Starting a dog walking service means that you are your own boss. You have the freedom to set your own schedule, choose your own clients, and make your own decisions. You can also work from home or from anywhere you choose.

Flexible Hours: Dog walking can be a flexible business. You decide whether to work part-time or full-time, depending on your availability and preferences. You can also schedule your walks around your other commitments, such as family, school, or other jobs.

Common Myths and Misconceptions about Dog Walking

Despite the many benefits of starting a dog walking service, there are still some common myths and misconceptions about dog walking. Here are some of the most common myths and misconceptions, and the truth behind them:

Myth: Dog Walking is Easy: Many people think that dog walking is an easy job that anyone can do. However, the truth is that dog walking can be challenging and demanding. You need to have physical stamina, knowledge of dog behavior, and the ability to handle several types of dogs. You also need to be prepared for unexpected situations, such as bad weather, emergencies, or aggressive dogs.

Myth: Dog Walking is Boring: Some people think that dog walking is a boring job that involves nothing more than walking dogs. However, the truth is that dog walking can be an exciting and varied experience. You get to explore different neighborhoods, parks, and trails. You also get to meet and interact with different dogs and their owners. Every day can be a new adventure.

Myth: Dog Walking is Low-Paying: Another common myth is that dog walking is a low-paying job that cannot provide a decent income. However, the truth is that dog walking can be a profitable business. With the right pricing and marketing strategies, you can charge competitive rates for your services and attract a steady stream of clients. You can also increase your earnings by offering additional services or expanding your business.

Demand and Potential of Dog Walking

The demand and potential of dog walking is high. Here are some statistics and facts that demonstrate the demand and potential of dog walking:

Number of Dog Owners: There are millions of dog owners in the United States alone. According to the American Pet Products Association, approximately 63.4 million households in the United States own a dog. This means that there is a large and growing market for dog walking services.

Average Spending on Pet Services: Dog owners spend a significant amount of money on pet services, including dog walking. According to the American Pet Products Association, the average annual spending on pet services, such as grooming and boarding, is $73 per household. This means that there is a significant potential for revenue from dog walking services.

Growth Rate of the Industry: The pet services industry, including dog walking, is growing at a steady rate. According to IBISWorld, the pet grooming and boarding industry in the United States has grown at an annual rate of 4.3% from 2015 to 2020. This means that there is a growing demand for dog walking services.

Success Stories and Testimonials from Dog Walkers

Many dog walkers have made a living or even a fortune from their business. Here are some success stories and testimonials from dog walkers who have achieved success with their dog walking service:

Success Story 1: Jane started her dog walking service as a side hustle while she was working a full-time job. She started by walking dogs in her neighborhood and gradually expanded her client base through word-of-mouth and referrals. Within a year, she was able to quit her full-time job and focus on her dog walking service full-time. She now has a team of dog walkers and offers additional services, such as pet sitting and dog training. She makes a six-figure income from her dog walking service.

Success Story 2: John was a college student when he started his dog walking service. He needed a flexible job that would allow him to attend classes and study. He started by walking dogs in his college town and quickly gained a reputation as a reliable and trustworthy dog walker. He was able to pay for his college tuition and expenses with the income from his dog walking service. After graduation, he continued to grow his dog walking service and now has a successful business with multiple employees.

Success Story 3: Sarah was a stay-at-home mom when she started her dog walking service. She wanted to earn some extra income while taking care of her children. She started by walking dogs in her neighborhood and soon discovered that there was a high demand for her services. She was able to balance her dog walking schedule with her family responsibilities and make a steady income from her dog walking service. She now has a thriving business and has even expanded to offer pet sitting and dog grooming services.

These stories and testimonials demonstrate that starting a dog walking service can be a rewarding and profitable experience. With the right planning, marketing, and operations, you can turn your love for dogs into a successful business.

HOW TO PLAN YOUR DOG WALKING SERVICE

This chapter will guide you through the planning process of your dog walking service. Planning is an essential step in starting any business, and a dog walking service is no exception. By taking the time to plan, you can set yourself up for success and prevent common pitfalls. In this chapter, you will learn how to set your goals, choose your niche, define your target market, research your competition, and determine your pricing and services. You will also learn how to create a business name, logo, slogan, and brand identity for your dog walking service. Additionally, this chapter will advise you on the legal and financial aspects of your business, such as registering your business, obtaining licenses and permits, getting insurance, opening a bank account, and keeping records. Finally, you will be provided with a checklist of the equipment and supplies you will need for your dog walking service, such as leashes, collars, harnesses, poop bags, treats, water bottles, and first aid kits.

Setting Your Goals

The first step in planning your dog walking service is to set your goals. What do you want to achieve with your business? Do you want to make a full-time income, or are you looking for a side hustle to supplement your existing income? Do you want to work with a specific breed or size of dog, or are you open to working with all types of dogs? Do you want to offer additional services, such as pet sitting or dog training? By setting clear and specific goals, you can focus your efforts and make decisions that will help you achieve those goals.

One way to set your goals is to use the SMART criteria. **SMART** stands for **S**pecific, **M**easurable, **A**ttainable, **R**elevant, and **T**ime-bound. By setting SMART goals, you can ensure that your goals are clear, achievable, and aligned with your overall vision for your business. For example, a SMART goal for your dog walking service might be: 'To earn $1,000 per month from dog walking services within the first six months of starting my business.' This goal is specific (earn $1,000 per month), measurable (you can track your income), attainable (it is a realistic goal), relevant (it is related to your business), and time-bound (you have set a deadline of six months).

Choosing Your Niche

The next step in planning your dog walking service is to choose your niche. A niche is a specific area of focus or specialization within a larger market. By choosing a niche, you can differentiate yourself from your competition and attract a specific type of customer. For example, you might choose to specialize in working with large breeds, such as Great Danes or Mastiffs. Or you might choose to focus on providing dog walking services to senior citizens or busy professionals. By choosing a niche, you can tailor your marketing and services to meet the needs and preferences of your target market.

To choose your niche, you can start by researching the dog walking market in your area. What types of dog walking services are already available? Is there demand in the market that you can fill? You can also survey potential customers to find out what they are looking for in a dog walking service. By understanding the needs and preferences of your target market, you can choose a niche that will help you attract and retain customers.

Defining Your Target Market

Once you have chosen your niche, the next step is to define your target market. Your target market is the group of customers that you want to attract and serve with your dog walking service. By effectively defining this market, you can tailor your marketing and services to meet your customer's needs. For example, if your target market is senior citizens, you might offer a slower-paced walk or a discount for regular customers. Or, if your target market is busy professionals, you might offer early morning or late evening walks to accommodate their schedules.

To define your target market, you can start by creating a customer profile. A customer profile is a detailed description of your ideal customer, including their demographics (age, gender, income, etc.), psychographics (values, beliefs, interests, etc.), and behaviors (how they make decisions, what they look for in a dog walking service, etc.). By creating a customer profile, you can gain a deeper understanding of your target market and how to attract and serve them.

Researching Your Competition

Another crucial step in planning your dog walking service is to research your competition. By understanding your competition, you can identify their strengths and weaknesses and find ways to differentiate yourself from them. For example, you might offer a unique service, such as dog hiking or dog yoga, which sets you apart from your competition. Or you might offer a loyalty program or referral program to incentivize customers to choose your dog walking service over your competition.

To research your competition, you can start by conducting a competitive analysis. A competitive analysis is a detailed evaluation of your competition, including their services, pricing, marketing, and customer reviews. By conducting a competitive analysis, you can gain valuable insights into your competition and how to position your dog walking service in the market.

Determining Your Pricing and Services

Once you have set your goals, chosen your niche, defined your target market, and researched your competition, the next step is to determine your pricing and services. Your pricing and services are two of the most important factors that will influence the success of your dog walking service. By setting the right prices and offering the right services, you can attract and retain customers and generate a steady income from your business.

To determine your pricing, you can start by researching the market rates for dog walking services in your area. You can also survey potential customers to find out how much they are willing to pay for dog walking services. Based on your research, you can set your prices at a competitive level that will attract customers and generate a profit for your business. You can also consider offering discounts or promotions to attract new customers or incentivize repeat business.

To determine your services, you can start by thinking about what your target market is looking for in a dog walking service. Do they want a basic walk, or are they looking for additional services, such as pet sitting or dog training? Based on your research, you can decide which services to offer and how to package and price them. You can also consider offering add-on services, such as feeding or administering medication, to provide additional value to your customers.

Creating a Business Name, Logo, Slogan, and Brand Identity

Another crucial step in planning your dog walking service is to create a business name, logo, slogan, and brand identity. Your business name, logo, slogan, and brand identity are the public face of your business. They represent who you are, what you do, and why you are different from your competition. By creating a strong and memorable business name, logo, slogan, and brand identity, you can attract and retain customers and build a loyal following for your dog walking service.

To create a business name, you can start by brainstorming a list of potential names. You can use your own name, the name of your city or neighborhood, or a descriptive word or phrase that represents your business. You can also use a business name generator tool, such as Namelix or Oberlo, to generate a list of potential names. Once you have a list of potential names, you can narrow it down by checking for availability, trademark issues, and domain name availability. You can also survey potential customers to get their feedback on your potential names.

To create a logo, you can start by sketching out some ideas or using a logo maker tool, such as Canva or Looka, to generate some potential designs. Your logo should be simple, memorable, and representative of your business. You can also hire a graphic designer to create a custom logo for your business.

To create a slogan, you can start by thinking about what makes your dog walking service unique or different from your competition. Your slogan should be short, catchy, and memorable. It should also convey the main benefit or value that your dog walking service offers to your customers. You can also use a slogan generator tool, such as Sloganizer or Shopify, to generate some potential slogans.

To create a brand identity, you can start by defining your brand values, personality, and voice. Your brand values are the core beliefs and principles that guide your business. Your brand personality is the human-like traits and characteristics that represent your business. Your brand voice is the tone and style of your communication. By defining your brand values, personality, and voice, you can create a consistent and authentic brand identity that will attract and retain customers.

Legal and Financial Aspects of Your Business

Another major step in planning your dog walking service is to address the legal and financial aspects of your business. By taking care of the legal and financial aspects of your business, you can protect yourself and your business from potential risks and liabilities. In this section, you will learn how to register your business, obtain licenses and permits, get insurance, open a bank account, and keep records.

To register your business, you will need to choose a business structure, such as a sole proprietorship, partnership, LLC, or corporation. Each business structure has its own advantages and disadvantages, and the right choice will depend on your specific circumstances and goals. You can research the different business structures and consult with a lawyer or accountant to determine the best option for your business. Once you have chosen a business structure, you can register your business with your state or local government.

To obtain licenses and permits, you will need to research the requirements for dog walking services in your area. Some states or cities may require a general business license, while others may require a specific license or permit for dog walking services. You can research the requirements for your area and apply for the necessary licenses and permits. You may also need to obtain a sales tax permit if you are required to collect sales tax on your services.

To get insurance, you will need to research the different types of insurance that are available for dog walking services. Some common types of insurance for dog walking services include general liability insurance, professional liability insurance, and workers' compensation insurance. You can research several types of insurance and consult with an insurance agent to determine the best coverage for your business. By obtaining the right insurance, you can protect yourself and your business from potential risks and liabilities.

To open a bank account, you will need to choose a bank and provide the necessary documentation, such as your business registration and tax ID number. You can research the different banks and their business account options to find the best fit for your business. By opening a business bank account, you can keep your personal and business finances separate and make it easier to manage your business finances.

To keep records, you will need to set up a system for tracking your income and expenses, as well as your clients and services. You can use a spreadsheet or accounting software to track your finances, and CRM or scheduling software to track your clients and services. By keeping accurate and organized records, you can make informed decisions about your business and prepare for tax time.

Equipment and Supplies Checklist

The last step in planning your dog walking service is to create a checklist of the equipment and supplies you will need. By having the right equipment and supplies, you can provide a high-quality service to your customers and ensure the safety and wellbeing of the dogs in your care. Here is a checklist of the equipment and supplies you will need for your dog walking service:

Poop bags: You will need poop bags to clean up after the dogs in your care. You can choose biodegradable poop bags to reduce your environmental impact.

Treats: You may want to carry treats with you to reward good behavior or to use as a training tool. Make sure to check with the dog's owner before giving any treats, as some dogs may have dietary restrictions.

Water bottles: You will need to carry water with you, especially on hot days, to ensure that the dogs in your care stay hydrated. You can use a collapsible water bowl or a water bottle with a built-in bowl to make it easy to give the dogs water while on the go.

First aid kit: It is a great idea to carry a first aid kit with you in case of emergencies. The first aid kit should include bandages, antiseptic wipes, and tweezers. You may also want to take a pet first aid course to learn how to handle common emergencies.

By having this essential equipment and supplies, you can provide a professional and reliable dog walking service for your customers.

HOW TO MARKET YOUR DOG WATCHING SERVICE

Marketing is a crucial aspect of any business, and a dog walking service is no exception. In this chapter, you will learn how to effectively market your dog walking service to attract and retain customers. You will learn how to create a website, social media pages, flyers, business cards, and brochures to promote your business. You will also learn how to use online and offline strategies to reach your target market, including search engine optimization (SEO), online directories, referrals, word-of-mouth, networking, partnerships, and events. Additionally, this chapter will help you create a marketing plan and budget for your dog walking service, as well as how to measure and evaluate your marketing results.

Creating a website

One of the first steps in marketing your dog walking service is to create a website. A website serves as the online home for your business, providing potential customers with information about your services, pricing, and contact information. A well-designed and user-friendly website can help you attract and retain customers, as well as establish credibility and professionalism.

To create a website, you can use a website builder tool, such as Wix or Squarespace, to design and publish your website. These tools provide templates and drag-and-drop interfaces that make it easy to create a professional-looking website without any coding or design skills. Alternatively, hire a web designer to create a custom website for your business.

When creating your website, be sure to include the following information:

Services: Provide a detailed description of the services you offer, including the length and frequency of the walks, the number of dogs you can walk at once, and any additional services, such as pet sitting or dog training.

Pricing: Clearly display your pricing for each service, including any discounts or promotions you may offer. Be sure to explain how your pricing is competitive and provides value to your customers.

About: Include a section about yourself and your business, including your experience, qualifications, and passion for dogs. This can help establish trust and credibility with potential customers.

Contact: Provide clear and easy-to-find contact information, including your phone number, email address, and physical address (if applicable). You may also want to include a contact form to make it easy for potential customers to contact you.

Using Social Media

Social media is another powerful tool for marketing your dog walking service. By creating and maintaining social media pages for your business, you can reach a large and engaged audience of potential customers. Social media platforms, such as Facebook, Instagram, and Twitter, allow you to share photos, videos, and updates about your business, as well as interact with your followers and build a community around your brand.

To use social media effectively, be sure to follow these best practices:

Choose the right platforms: Not all social media platforms are created equal. Choose the platforms that are most popular with your target market and where you can best highlight your business. For example, Instagram is a great platform for sharing photos of the dogs you walk, while Facebook is a good platform for sharing updates and promotions.

Post regularly: To keep your followers engaged and interested in your business, be sure to post regularly on your social media pages. Aim for at least one post per day and vary the content to keep it interesting.

Use hashtags: Hashtags are a powerful tool for increasing the visibility of your posts on social media. Use relevant and popular hashtags, such as #dogwalking or #dogsofinstagram, to help your posts reach a wider audience.

Engage with your followers: Social media is a two-way conversation. Be sure to respond to comments and messages from your followers, and engage with them by asking questions, running polls, or hosting giveaways. This can help build a loyal and engaged community around your brand.

Creating Flyers, Business Cards, and Brochures

In addition to online marketing, you can also use offline marketing materials, such as flyers, business cards, and brochures, to promote your dog walking service. These materials can be distributed in your local area to reach potential customers who may not be active on social media or who prefer more traditional forms of advertising.

To create effective flyers, business cards, and brochures, be sure to follow these best practices:

Use eye-catching design: Your marketing materials should be visually appealing and eye-catching to grab the attention of potential customers. Use bright colors, bold fonts, and high-quality images to make your materials stand out.

Include the most essential information: Your marketing materials should include the most valuable information about your business, such as your services, pricing, and contact information. Keep the text concise and easy to read and use bullet points or lists to organize the information.

Include a call to action: Your marketing materials should include a clear and compelling call to action, such as 'Call now to book your first walk' or 'Visit our website for more information.' This can help motivate potential customers to act and contact you.

Using Online and Offline Strategies

In addition to creating a website, using social media, and creating flyers, business cards, and brochures, there are many other online and offline strategies you can use to market your dog walking service. These strategies can help you reach a wider audience and attract more customers to your business.

Some effective online and offline strategies include:

Search engine optimization (SEO): SEO is the process of improving the visibility of your website in search engine results pages. By optimizing your website for relevant keywords, such as 'dog walking' or 'dog walking service,' you can increase the chances of potential customers finding your website when they search for dog walking services in your area.

Online directories: Online directories, such as Yelp or Google My Business, allow you to create a listing for your dog walking service. These directories can help potential customers find your business when they search for dog walking services in your area. Be sure to include detailed information about your business, including your services, pricing, and contact information, as well as photos and customer reviews.

Referrals: Referrals are a powerful way to attract new customers to your dog walking service. Encourage your existing customers to refer friends and family to your business by offering incentives, such as a discount or free walks. Word-of-mouth is a powerful marketing tool, and a referral from a satisfied customer can be more effective than any advertisement.

Networking: Networking with other pet-related businesses, such as veterinarians, pet stores, or groomers, can help you reach new customers. Attending local pet-related events, join pet-related associations, or partner with other pet-related businesses to cross-promote your services.

Creating a Marketing Plan and Budget

To effectively market your dog walking service, it is important to create a marketing plan and budget. A marketing plan outlines the strategies and tactics you will use to reach your target market and attract customers to your business. A marketing budget allocates the resources and expenses for your marketing efforts.

To create a marketing plan, start by defining your marketing goals. What do you want to achieve with your marketing efforts? Do you want to increase awareness of your business, attract new customers, or retain existing customers? Once you have defined your marketing goals, you can choose the strategies and tactics that will help you achieve those goals. For example, if your goal is to attract new customers, you might focus on SEO, online directories, and referrals.

To create a marketing budget, start by determining how much you can afford to spend on marketing. This will depend on your overall business budget and the stage of your business. If you are just starting out, you may have a smaller marketing budget than an established business. Once you have determined your marketing budget, you can allocate the funds to the strategies and tactics that will provide the best return on investment. For example, if you have a limited budget, you might focus on low-cost or free marketing strategies, such as social media or referrals.

Measuring and Evaluating Your Marketing Results

Finally, it is important to measure and evaluate your marketing results to determine the effectiveness of your marketing efforts. By tracking your marketing results, you can identify what is working and what is not and make data-driven decisions to improve your marketing efforts.

To measure and evaluate your marketing results, start by defining your key performance indicators (KPIs). KPIs are the metrics that you will use to measure the success of your marketing efforts. For example, if your goal is to attract new customers, your KPIs might include the number of new customers, the cost per acquisition, or the conversion rate. Once you have defined your KPIs, you can track and analyze your marketing results to determine the effectiveness of your marketing efforts. You can use tools, such as Google Analytics or CRM, to track your marketing results and generate reports to help you make data-driven decisions.

In conclusion, marketing is a crucial aspect of any dog walking service. By following the steps outlined in this chapter, you can effectively market your dog walking service to attract and retain customers. Remember to create a website, use social media, create flyers, business cards, and brochures, and use online and offline strategies to reach your target market. Additionally, be sure to create a marketing plan and budget, and measure and evaluate your marketing results to continuously improve your marketing efforts.

HOW TO OPERATE YOUR DOG WALKING SERVICE

In this chapter, you will learn how to operate your dog walking service. Operating a dog walking service involves managing the day-to-day tasks and responsibilities of running your business. This includes scheduling, booking, invoicing, collecting payments, and communicating with clients. Additionally, this chapter will teach you how to provide a high-quality service, including meeting and greeting the dogs and owners, preparing for the walk, choosing the route, handling the dogs, and ending the walk. You will also learn tips and tricks on how to deal with common issues and challenges, such as bad weather, emergencies, injuries, illnesses, lost dogs, aggressive dogs, and unhappy clients.

Scheduling

Scheduling is an important aspect of operating a dog walking service. You need to manage your time effectively to ensure that you can meet the needs of your clients and provide a reliable service. To manage your schedule, you can use a paper planner, an online calendar, or scheduling software. These tools can help you keep track of your appointments, set reminders, and avoid double-booking. When scheduling your walks, be sure to allow enough time for travel, preparation, and rest between walks. You should also consider the needs and preferences of your clients, such as their preferred time and frequency of walks.

Booking

Booking is another important aspect of operating a dog walking service. You need to have a system in place for accepting and managing bookings from your clients. This can include making bookings by phone, email, or through your website. You should have a clear and consistent booking process, including a booking form that collects all the necessary information, such as the client's name, contact details, and the dog's information. You should also have a cancellation policy in place, such as requiring 24 hours' notice for cancellations or charging a cancellation fee. By having a clear and consistent booking process, you can provide a professional and reliable service to your clients.

Invoicing and Collecting Payments

Invoicing and collecting payments are essential tasks for any business, including a dog walking service. You need to have a system in place for issuing invoices and collecting payments from your clients. This can include sending invoices by email, mail, or through online invoicing software. You should have clear and consistent payment terms, such as requiring payment within 14 days of the invoice date. You should also offer a variety of payment methods, such as cash, check, credit card, or online payment. By having a clear and consistent invoicing and payment process, you can ensure that you get paid on time and maintain a healthy cash flow for your business.

Communicating with Clients

Communicating with clients is a crucial aspect of operating a dog walking service. You need to keep your clients informed and updated about their dog walks, as well as respond to any questions or concerns they may have. This can include sending regular updates by text, email, or through a mobile app. You should also be available to answer any questions or concerns your clients may have, either by phone, email, or in person. By maintaining open and regular communication with your clients, you can build trust and loyalty, and ensure their satisfaction with your service.

Providing a High-Quality Service

Providing a high-quality service is essential for the success of your dog walking service. You need to ensure that you meet the needs and expectations of your clients and provide a safe and enjoyable experience for their dogs. This includes meeting and greeting the dogs and owners, preparing for the walk, choosing the route, handling the dogs, and ending the walk. You should also be prepared to deal with any issues or challenges that may arise, such as bad weather, emergencies, injuries, illnesses, lost dogs, aggressive dogs, or unhappy clients.

When meeting and greeting the dogs and owners, be sure to introduce yourself and your business, and ask any questions you may have about the dog's behavior, health, or preferences. You should also provide the owner with any information or instructions they may need, such as how to contact you or what to do in case of an emergency. When preparing for the walk, be sure to check the weather and dress appropriately, as well as pack any necessary equipment or supplies, such as leashes, collars, harnesses, poop bags, treats, water bottles, and first aid kits.

When choosing the route, consider the needs and preferences of the dog, as well as the safety and accessibility of the route. You may want to vary the route to keep the walks interesting and stimulating for the dog. When handling the dogs, be sure to use positive reinforcement techniques, such as praise and treats, to encourage good behavior. You should also be prepared to deal with any issues or challenges that may arise, such as pulling on the leash, barking, or aggression towards other dogs or people. When ending the walk, be sure to return the dog safely to their home, provide them with water and a treat (if allowed), and update the owner on the walk.

Dealing with Common Issues and Challenges

Operating a dog walking service can come with its share of issues and challenges. You need to be prepared to deal with common issues, such as severe weather, emergencies, injuries, illnesses, lost dogs, aggressive dogs, and unhappy clients. By being prepared and having a plan in place, you can minimize the impact of these issues and provide a professional and reliable service to your clients.

In case of harsh weather, such as rain, snow, or extreme heat, you should have a plan in place for how to handle the situation. This may include rescheduling the walk, shortening the walk, or providing an alternative indoor activity for the dog. In case of an emergency, such as an injury or illness, you should have a first aid kit and know how to administer basic first aid. You should also have the contact information for the dog's veterinarian and the owner's emergency contact. In case of a lost dog, you should have a plan in place for how to search for the dog and notify the owner. In the case of an aggressive dog, you should know how to handle the situation safely and calmly, with a plan in place to prevent future incidents. In case of an unhappy client, you should listen to their concerns, apologize for any mistakes, and offer a solution or compensation to resolve the issue.

In conclusion, operating a dog walking service involves managing the day-to-day tasks and responsibilities of running your business. By following the steps outlined in this chapter, you can effectively operate your dog walking service and provide a high-quality service to your clients. Remember to manage your schedule, bookings, invoicing, and payments, as well as communicate regularly with your clients. Additionally, be sure to provide a high-quality service, including meeting and greeting the dogs and owners, preparing for the walk, choosing the route, handling the dogs, and ending the walk. Finally, be prepared to deal with common issues and challenges, such as dangerous weather, emergencies, injuries, illnesses, lost dogs, aggressive dogs, and unhappy clients.

HOW TO GROW YOUR DOG WALKING SERVICE

Once you have established your dog walking service and have a steady stream of clients, you may want to consider growing your business. Growing your dog walking service can increase your income, expand your reach, and provide new opportunities for you and your business. In this chapter, you will learn how to grow your dog walking service by increasing your client base, expanding your service area, adding new services, hiring employees, and outsourcing tasks. You will also learn how to improve your skills and knowledge, set new goals and challenges, and continue to provide a high-quality service to your clients.

Increasing Your Client Base

One way to grow your dog walking service is to increase your client base. By attracting new clients to your business, you can increase your income and expand your reach. There are several ways to increase your client base, including:

Referrals: Encourage existing clients to refer their friends and family to your business. You can offer incentives, such as a discount or free walk, to clients who refer new business to you. Referrals are a powerful way to attract new customers, as people are more likely to trust the recommendation of someone they know. To encourage referrals, you can create a referral program that rewards your existing clients for bringing in new business. For example, you could offer a free walk for every new client they refer, or a discount on their next service. Make sure to promote your referral program to your existing clients and remind them of the benefits of referring their friends and family.

Marketing: Continue to market your business to attract new clients. This can include online and offline marketing strategies, such as social media, flyers, and business cards. Marketing is essential for any business, and a dog walking service is no exception. By creating a strong and consistent marketing message, you can attract new customers to your business. There are many different marketing strategies you can use, including online advertising, content marketing, email marketing, and event marketing. Choose the strategies that work best for your business and your target market and be sure to track and measure your results to see what is working and what is not.

Partnerships: Partner with other pet-related businesses, such as veterinarians, pet stores, or groomers, to cross-promote your services. This can help you reach new clients who may not have found your business otherwise. Partnerships can be a powerful way to grow your dog walking service. By partnering with other pet-related businesses, you can tap into their customer base and attract new clients to your business. For example, you could partner with a local pet store to offer a discount on dog walking services to their customers. Or you could partner with a local veterinarian to offer a joint package of dog walking and veterinary services. Be creative and think of ways to add value to your partners and their customers.

Expanding Your Service Area

Another way to grow your dog walking service is to expand your service area. By offering your services in new neighborhoods or cities, you can reach new clients and increase your income. When expanding your service area, be sure to research the market and competition in the new area to ensure that there is demand for your services. You may also need to obtain new licenses or permits to operate in the new area.

Expanding your service area can be a great way to grow your dog walking service. However, it is important to do your research and plan carefully before making the move. Start by researching the market in the new area to see if there is demand for dog walking services. Look at the competition to see what they are offering and how you can differentiate yourself. You may also need to obtain new licenses or permits to operate in the new area, so be sure to research the requirements and apply for any necessary licenses or permits.

Once you have done your research and planning, you can start to expand your service area. This may involve hiring new employees or contractors to cover the new area, or it may involve traveling to the new area yourself to provide the services. Be sure to promote your services in the new area, using marketing strategies such as flyers, social media, and partnerships with local businesses.

Adding New Services

Adding new services to your dog walking business can also help you grow. By offering additional services, such as pet sitting, dog training, or dog grooming, you can provide more value to your clients and increase your income. When adding new services, be sure to research the market and competition to ensure that there is demand for the new services. You may also need to obtain additional training or certifications to offer the new services.

Adding new services to your dog walking business can be a great way to grow your income and provide more value to your clients. However, it is important to do your research and planning before adding new services. Start by researching the market to see if there is demand for the new services. Look at the competition to see what they are offering and how you can differentiate yourself. You may also need to obtain additional training or certifications to offer the new services, so be sure to research the requirements and obtain any necessary training or certifications.

Once you have done your research and planning, you can start to add new services to your dog walking business. This may involve hiring new employees or contractors with the necessary skills and certifications, or it may involve obtaining the training or certifications yourself. Be sure to promote your new services to your existing clients and to potential new clients, using marketing strategies such as email marketing, social media, and partnerships with local businesses.

Hiring Employees

As your dog walking business grows, you may need to hire employees to help you manage the increased workload. Hiring employees can help you expand your service area, offer more services, and serve more clients. When hiring employees, be sure to follow all legal and financial requirements, such as obtaining workers' compensation insurance and withholding taxes. You should also provide training and support to your employees to ensure that they provide a high-quality service to your clients.

Hiring employees can be a big step for any business, and a dog walking service is no exception. Before hiring employees, be sure to do your research and planning to ensure that you are ready to take on the responsibilities of being an employee. Start by researching the legal and financial requirements for hiring employees, such as obtaining workers' compensation insurance and withholding taxes. You may also need to register as an employer with your state or federal government and obtain an employer identification number (EIN).

Once you have done your research and planning, you can start to hire employees for your dog walking service. This may involve posting job ads, screening resumes, conducting interviews, and checking references. Be sure to choose employees who are dependable, trustworthy, and passionate about dogs. You should also provide training and support to your employees to ensure that they provide a high-quality service to your clients. This may include training on dog behavior, first aid, and customer service.

Outsourcing Tasks

Another way to grow your dog walking business is to outsource tasks that are not core to your business. By outsourcing tasks, such as bookkeeping, marketing, or website design, you can free up your time to focus on providing a high-quality service to your clients. When outsourcing tasks, be sure to choose reputable and reliable service providers who can provide the services you need at a reasonable cost.

Outsourcing tasks can be a great way to free up your time and focus on the core aspects of your dog walking business. However, it is important to choose the right service providers and manage the outsourcing process effectively. Start by identifying the tasks that you want to outsource, such as bookkeeping, marketing, or website design. Then, research potential service providers to find the ones that can provide the services you need at a reasonable cost. Be sure to check their references and reviews to ensure that they are reputable and reliable.

Once you have chosen your service providers, you can start to outsource tasks to them. Be sure to communicate your needs and expectations clearly and provide any necessary information or materials. You should also monitor the outsourcing process to ensure that the tasks are completed to your satisfaction. By outsourcing tasks effectively, you can free up your time to focus on growing your dog walking business.

Improving Your Skills and Knowledge

As you grow your dog walking business, it is important to continue to improve your skills and knowledge. By staying up to date with the latest trends and best practices in the dog walking industry, you can provide a better service to your clients and stay ahead of your competition.

There are several ways to improve your skills and knowledge, including:

Courses: Take courses or workshops to learn new skills or techniques related to dog walking, such as dog behavior, first aid, or business management. There are many courses and workshops available, both online and offline, that can help you improve your skills and knowledge. Look for courses that are relevant to your business and that are instructed by reputable and experienced instructors. By taking courses and workshops, you can learn new skills and techniques that will help you provide a better service to your clients.

Books: Read books or articles about dog walking or pet care to stay informed about the latest trends and best practices. There are many books and articles available about dog walking and pet care. Look for books and articles that are written by experts in the field and that provide practical and actionable advice. By reading books and articles, you can stay up to date with the latest trends and best practices in the dog walking industry.

Associations: Join a professional association for dog walkers or pet care providers to network with other professionals and access resources and training opportunities. There are several professional associations for dog walkers and pet care providers, both at the national and local level. By joining a professional association, you can network with other professionals, access resources and training opportunities, and stay up to date with the best practices in the dog walking industry.

Setting New Goals and Challenges

As you grow your dog walking business, it is important to continue to set new goals and challenges for yourself and your business. By setting new goals, you can continue to push yourself and your business to achieve more. Some new goals and challenges you might set for your dog walking business include:

Expanding to new markets or locations: You might set a goal to expand your dog walking service to new neighborhoods, cities, or even states. This can help you reach new customers and increase your revenue.

Offering new or specialized services: You might set a goal to offer new or specialized services, such as dog training, pet sitting, or pet transportation. This can help you differentiate yourself from your competition and provide more value to your customers.

Increasing revenue or profitability: You might set a goal to increase your revenue or profitability by a certain percentage or amount. This can help you measure the success of your business and make data-driven decisions to improve your operations.

Improving customer satisfaction or retention: You might set a goal to improve your customer satisfaction or retention rates. This can help build a loyal customer base, generating repeat business.

Developing a strong brand or reputation: You might set a goal to develop a strong brand or reputation for your dog walking service. This can help you attract new customers and establish yourself as a leader in the dog walking industry.

HOW TO SUCCEED AS A DOG WALKER

In this book, we have covered the essential steps to starting, operating, and growing a successful dog walking service. From planning and marketing to providing a high-quality service and dealing with common challenges, we have provided you with the knowledge and tools you need to succeed as a dog walker.

But success as a dog walker is not just about following the steps outlined in this book. It also requires passion, dedication, and a willingness to learn and grow. Here are some key takeaways to help you succeed as a dog walker:

Love what you do: Passion is the key to success in any business, and dog walking is no exception. If you love dogs and enjoy spending time with them, you are more likely to succeed as a dog walker. Your passion will shine through in the quality of your service, and your clients will appreciate the care and attention you give to their furry friends. Loving what you do also means that you will be more motivated to provide the best service possible, and to continuously improve and grow your business.

Be professional: As a dog walker, you are running a business, and it is important to always act professionally. This means being reliable, punctual, and organized, as well as communicating effectively with your clients. By being professional, you can build trust and credibility with your clients, and establish a reputation as a reliable and trustworthy dog walker. Professionalism also means taking care of the legal and financial aspects of your business, such as registering your business, obtaining licenses and permits, getting insurance, and keeping accurate records.

Never stop learning: The dog walking industry is constantly evolving, and it is important to stay up to date with the latest trends and best practices. This means continuing to learn and improve your skills, whether through courses, books, or networking with other dog walkers. By staying informed and up to date, you can provide a better service to your clients and stay ahead of your competition. Continuous learning also means being open to feedback and suggestions from your clients and using that feedback to improve and grow your business.

Be adaptable: Running a dog walking service can come with its share of challenges, and it is important to be adaptable and able to deal with unexpected situations. This means being prepared for bad weather, emergencies, or difficult dogs, and having a plan in place to handle these situations. By being adaptable, you can provide a reliable and consistent service to your clients, even when things do not go as planned. Adaptability also means being open to change and willing to try new things, whether it is expanding your service area, offering new services, or experimenting with innovative marketing strategies.

Set goals and keep growing: As your dog walking business grows, it is important to continue to set new goals and challenges for yourself and your business. This means expanding into new markets, offering new services, or increasing your revenue. By setting goals and striving to achieve them, you can continue to grow and succeed as a dog walker. Setting goals also means regularly evaluating your progress and adjusting as needed to stay on track and achieve your desired outcomes.

In conclusion, success as a dog walker is within your reach. By following the steps outlined in this book, and by being passionate, professional, adaptable, and willing to learn and grow, you can build a successful and rewarding dog walking business. So go ahead and take the first step towards your dream of becoming a successful dog walker.

ABOUT THE AUTHOR

EmptyInkwell is an independent author and publisher of books that focus on practical ways to make money. With a passion for helping others achieve financial success, EmptyInkwell's books provide readers with actionable tips and strategies for generating extra income through simple side hustles. Through their writing, EmptyInkwell empowers readers to take control of their financial future and achieve their goals.

www.ingramcontent.com/pod-product-compliance
Lightning Source LLC
Chambersburg PA
CBHW070955220526
45471CB00007B/3044